THE
Old Photographs
SERIES

DOVER

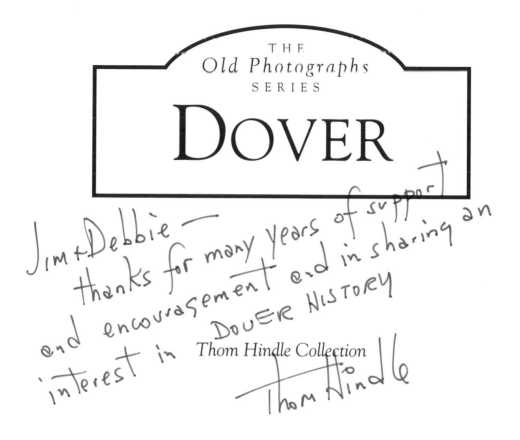

THE Old Photographs SERIES

DOVER

Jim + Debbie —
thanks for many years of support
and encouragement and in sharing an
interest in DOVER HISTORY

Thom Hindle Collection

Thom Hindle

ALAN SUTTON

BATH • AUGUSTA • RENNES

First published 1994
Copyright © Thom Hindle, 1994

ISBN 0 7524 0067 3

Published by Alan Sutton, Inc., Augusta, Maine.
Distributed by Berwick Publishing, Inc.,
1 Washington Street, Dover, New Hampshire 03820.
Printed in Great Britain.

Contents

Century of Change

During the mid-1800s, the Landing was the center of activity in Dover as large schooners moved tons of cargo in and out of the city. On 1 March, 1896, the date known as Dover's Black Day, large chunks of ice tore apart the Central Avenue Bridge. Buildings and businesses were carried over the dam and into the landing, destroying many operations on the river and becoming a contributing factor in the closing of the river to schooner shipping forever. Dover already had three railroads being serviced by nine stations, and automobiles were about to replace the horse and carriage. By 1914, the Dover Navigation Company was dissolved and the landing was never the same as daily activity moved to Tuttle, Central and Franklin Squares.

There have been many physical changes in the growing landscape of Dover since the turn of the century. The photographs appearing in this book are a record of some of those changes, as recorded by Dover photographers from the 1890s to the present. These images give us a glimpse of our city as our grandparents saw it, refresh memories for those of us who grew up in Dover during the 1930s, '40s and '50s, and will be a visual reference to the past for future generations who will see another Century of Change.

Why did it tell a lie on Washington's birthday?

To the day traveller, as well as the nocturnal pilgrim, the opera house clock has generally appeared sober and honest. It has been consoling to see the hour, and companionable to note the face of such a friend, especially when the friend properly extended his hands.

Yesterday, the birthday of the man who never told a lie, the city's clock lost its reputation. All day long it towered above us with a flaunting falsehood on its face. For the sake of suffering community, we earnestly call upon the mayor to start the clock.

> Mayor, start that clock,
> For the time we cannot see;
> It can't be more than twelve,
> And yet it looks like three.

If the clock is incapable of managing the works with which it is entitled, imitate Ike Lucas by putting on an extra hand.

> Is it half after twelve,
> or six or eight or two?
> These sort of keeping city hours
> No kind of good can do.

By John B. Stevens, Jr.
Dover, N.H.
23 February, 1898.

Dover City Hall Opera House was dedicated on 16 December, 1891. Governor Charles Sawyer called it 'The People's Palace.'

Built at a cost of $175,000, the Opera House featured a seating capacity of 1,500, a rising and falling floor, and three tiered balconies with velvet curtains and brass rails. Moving pictures were shown as early as 1896. In addition to big names including John Phillips Sousa's band, many of Dover's local talent performed in school plays, minstrel shows and city functions here.

City Opera House.

DOVER, N. H.

The Annual Bal Masque,
By Kankamagus Tribe, No. 2.

Friday Evening, ... Dec. 30, 1898.

Orchestra.

Retain this Check.

December 30.

Orchestra.

C 173
RIGHT.

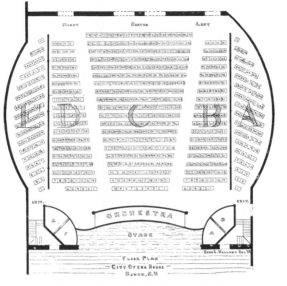

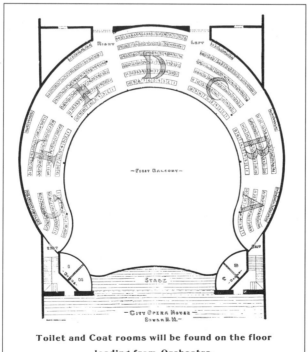

**Toilet and Coat rooms will be found on the floor
leading from Orchestra.**

The present City Hall is a Georgian Colonial building designed by J.E. Richardson of Dover in 1935. One million bricks and 190 tons of steel were used to construct the fireproof City Hall. Sixteen fireproof vaults were installed to protect city records. The total cost was $300,000. Interior and exterior renovations have been made in recent years.

One

Merchants

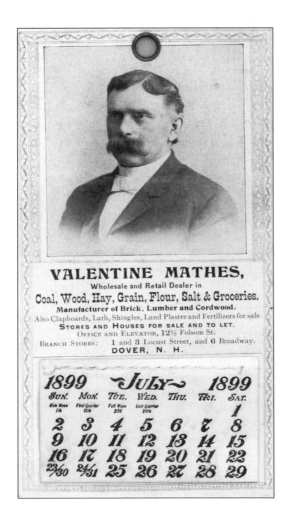

Central Square

The intersection where Central Avenue crosses Washington Street is called Central Square, but is often referred to as Lower Square. It was once a center for activity when the City Hall, a bank, the local newspapers, and numerous merchants were only footsteps from the mill gates.

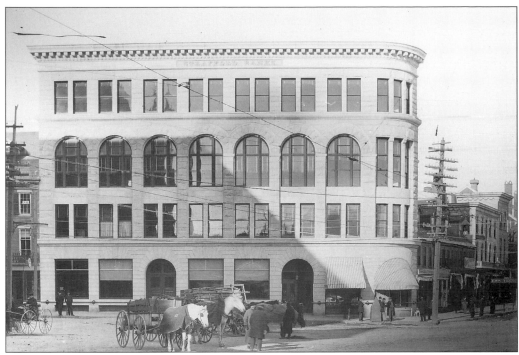

Known as the 'Fortress of Finance,' this notable architectural structure was designed by A.T. Ramsdell of Dover and constructed in 1895. It was built from Milford pink granite and stood four stories high. It was the original site of the Strafford Bank, which moved to the opposite corner of the intersection in the 1960s. Major interior renovations were made to accommodate office space.

These photographs show changes as seen in the early 1900s looking south toward the Opera House, and again in the 1940s with City Hall and a traffic island in the middle of the square.

Built on land purchased from the city, a Masonic Temple was built at the corner of Washington Street and Central Avenue in 1890. A fire on 29 March, 1906, completely destroyed the building. At a cost of $75,000, the building was rebuilt in 1907.

On 8 December, 1949, a rededication and consecration took place with both Strafford Lodge and Moses Paul Lodge hosting the ceremony. During the 1980s, major interior and storefront exterior renovations were made to the building, and in 1990 the Masonic Lodges moved from the building.

The King Building on the corner of Central Avenue and Orchard Street (above) at the turn of the century shows W.H. Vickery & Son, pharmacist. Note the photograph studio skylight window at the rear of the building. The c.1950s photograph below shows changes made to the rest of the block with little change to the King Building.

Merchants Row, as it was called during early mill days, has seen many businesses in the past century.

The National Block, erected in the early 1880s, had businesses like Dover Clothing Co., Dearborn Dry Goods (Newburys), and Charles Hodgon's Jewelry located in the space shown in the photograph as Kate's Style Shop.

These photographs show many familiar shop names during the 1940s.

→→STERNS'←←

European Passage and Exchange Office.

CABIN, INTERMEDIATE AND STEERAGE TICKETS · · · · · · ·
· · · · · · · · · · · · · · · · · BY ALL LINES AND AT LOWEST RATES.

MOSES W. STERNS, Manager, 386 Central Avenue.

DOVER, N. H., *Ap 26* 1890.

Memorandum of Issue of Draft. *White Star* Line_____

Number *20633* Amount £2———— $9.90/100

Payable to *John Morrison*

Purchaser *James Morrison* *M W S*

TO BE PRESENTED WITHIN SIX MONTHS FROM DATE OF ISSUE.

The E. Morrill Furniture Co. This building was founded by E. Morrill in 1843 at 93 Washington Street as a crockery and drapery store. From 1920 to 1940, it was located at the end of Third Street.

Purchased in 1957 by Thomas Monahan, Morrill Furniture remained on the bridge at this Central Avenue location until the Cocheco Mill plaza renovation.

The full service Dover Hardware store, run by the Stocklan family since the 1930s, stood downtown. This store also became part of the mill renovation.

This c.1914 photograph shows the Vickery Pharmacy located in the King Building. The Vickery family was in the pharmacy business from the turn of the century until the 1930s.

The M & M Food Store was also located in the King Building, as shown in this 1940s photograph, with Miss Liberty offering bakery samples. Liberty glasses were given free with a purchase.

'Ham the Hatter.' This business dates back to 1839, when it was founded by Amos Purington, father-in-law of Mr Ham. Re-established in 1859 under the name of Purington & Ham, in 1877 as 'Ham and Hatter' and in 1890 as John T.W. Ham & Co, 'Ham' was a dealer in hats, caps and furs. Currently the offices of the Spinelli Companies are housed here.

'Fried clams a Speciality.' A favorite eating place during the late 1930s and early 1940s was Hannons. It was located on the Central Avenue bridge.

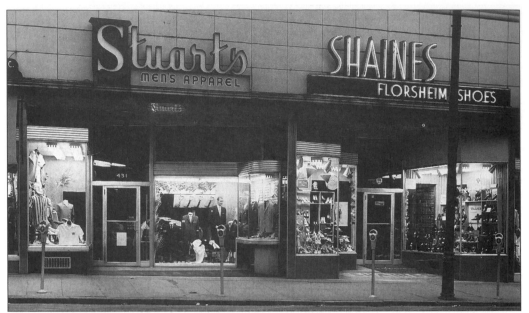

In May 1954, Edward and Stuart Shaines founded this shoe store. In 1957, it became a men's wear store. By 1967, the store had doubled in size. Stuart served a term as mayor in 1962/3.

Samuel King opened King's Jewelry in the 1950s. He had been in the jewelry business for many years. King's was located at 424 Central Avenue until 1979.

In the 1930s and '40s, Franklin Clothes was the place to buy Adams Hats. Located in Franklin Square, the store was destroyed by fire in December of 1951. W.T. Grant Co. later expanded into the space.

Montgomery Ward and W.T. Grant Co. operated side by side for many years in Dover. Wards is now located at the Newington Mall, and when W.T. Grant Co. closed in October 1967, the space was occupied by Morton's Clothing Store.

Franklin Square

The junction at Main Street and Central Avenue is considered Franklin Square, but has often been referred to as the Upper Square. After major renovations, the area was rechristened as Franklin Square in 1981. The original Morrill Block (left half) was built by Joseph Morrill on land purchased from the Cocheco Manufacturing Co. in 1844. Spofford-Allis Clothing was Dover's first chain store.

Between 1870 and 1874, Morrill erected this massive four-story wooden structure on the corner of Third Street. Fire destroyed the entire block on 3 January, 1932. A new stone Morrill Block was built as seen in this 1987 photo (below), taken just before renovations changed the building again in 1990.

Lothrops-Farnham Company was founded in 1854 with James E. Lothrop serving as president, Thomas Lothrop as clerk, and Charles H. Farnham as treasurer and manager. J.E. Lothrop was also president of J.E. Lothrop Pharmacy and served as mayor of the city. Farnham's moved to the Bracewell Building on the Central Avenue bridge and continues to operate at that location today.

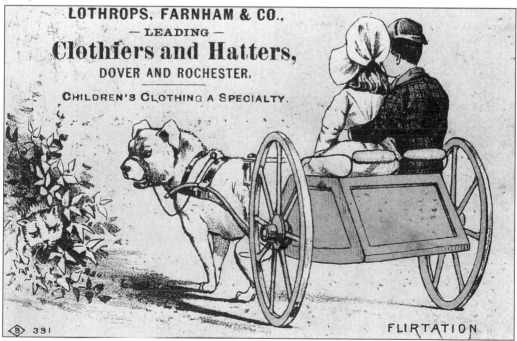

This is Franklin Square looking towards the Morrill Block with the Morrill Fountain. The tracks in the foreground carried the Atlantic Shore Line trollies to York.

This is a view looking from the end of Main Street into Franklin Square when horses shared the road with automobiles. Lothrop Piano Co. is in the foreground and the Freewill Baptist Church can be seen in the distance.

Alie's was founded in 1914 by Albert E. Alie. These photographs show the second store as it looked on the Morrill Block. Albert's grandson, Leo Alie, Jr., continues to operate at the same location in a newly expanded and remodeled store.

Winebaum's news store. Dover's popular news shop was located in the Morrill Block for half a century from the 1940s.

Detective magazines, daily newspapers, tobacco and cards were available seven days a week. The store was closed in 1991.

Winebaum's News was started in 1916 by Harry Winebaum, a sixteen-year-old newsboy. In the 1930s, Dover News operated from Depot Square on Third Street under the proprietorship of Thomas Winebaum, a wholesale news dealer.

The Ramble Inn lunch cart, operated by John Cullinane in the early 1900s, was converted to a diner in the 1950s. It was a popular eatery in Dover for many years. The Fish Shanty is now located on the site in the heart of Franklin Square.

Since the late 1800s, Lothrop Piano Store was another Franklin Square landmark. For many years, it was considered the largest piano store in New Hampshire. In the 1950s, the store was known as Lothrop Furniture.

Originally Harry Davis, a druggist, operated on the corner of Broadway at Central Avenue until Dover Drug was founded in 1920. The old Broadway theatre can be seen on Broadway. The storefront has gone through many changes as seen in the 1930s and 1940s photograph below.

A Walgreen Drug operated here (still called Dover Drug) in the late 1950s and then, in 1989, a major face lift was given to the front of the store. In 1991 the landmark Dover Drug sign was lowered and replaced with the current Brooks sign.

In October 1961 Mayor Pat Green (right) and Merchants Bank President Fred Easter (left), cut the ribbon for the opening of Squire's new men's store, located next to the American House.

A handsome three-and-a-half-story brick structure opened in June 1867 as 'The American.' President William Howard Taft addressed the city from the porch in 1912. This photograph dates from the 1930s.

Originally a horse trough given as a gift in 1914 by the heirs of Joseph Morrill, this fountain was rebuilt and rededicated in 1981 with water from Dover, England.

A turn-of-the-century cash grocery located at 5 Third Street, Redden Bros. Market provided meats, groceries and milk for 14 cents each in 1919.

REDDEN BROS.
CASH GROCERS
MEATS AND PROVISIONS

Dover, N. H. _Jan 16_ 1919

M _Mrs Hooper_

No.

Tel. Con.		5 Third St.	Reg. No.	Clerk

Am't Ord'd	Act'l Am't	Account Forwarded		
		Milk	14	25
		matches		4
		toilet Paper		30
		Steak		35
6		_oranges_		70
			15	84

REDDEN BROS.
CASH GROCERS
MEATS AND PROVISIONS

Dover, N. H. _Jan 16_ 191

M _Mrs Hooper_

No.

Tel. Con.		5 Third St.	Reg. No.	Clerk

Am't Ord'd	Act'l Am't	Account Forwarded		
		Milk	14	
		matches		
		toilet Paper		
		Steak		
		oranges		
			15	3

Daeris Tea Rooms was located in the original Morrill Block in the 1920s. It was relocated after the 1932 fire to the new Morrill Block as shown in this 1950s photograph. Famous for their soda fountain and candy counter, Daeris was destroyed by fire in 1959.

George Leighton ran the Hotel Leighton, Leighton Barbershop and Leighton's Lunch at 13 Third Street during the 1930s and '40s. It was famous for its Sunday 'One Dollar Turkey Dinners.'

The site where Varney's Cleaners now stands was Dover Furniture from 1890 to 1920; E. Morrill Furniture until 1940; then home to Greenlaw Furniture in 1948, and finally to Warren's Furniture until fire destroyed the building in 1975.

Ross Furniture, owned by R. Ross Rayeu, was established in 1942. On 12 September, 1946, the building was destroyed by fire. Rebuilt, it still operates on Third Street under the ownership of Bill Kafkas.

In April 1935, Mayor Keefe welcomed the Boston and Maine streamliner the 'Flying Yankee.' In 1944 the streamliner 'Mountaineer' was photographed in Dover. It travelled between Boston and Portland, with excursions to the White Mountains. In 1952 the 'Budliner' replaced the 'Streamliner' after twenty-two years of service.

Swift Provision was located at 11 Fourth Street from the early 1900s. It is now part of the Holmwood Furniture complex.

Chris Tsoronis the 'Hot Dog King' is seen in this 1950s snapshot with his early lunch wagon. Chris was a familiar lunch time sight at Dover High and on the avenue next to Dover Hardware every evening during the 1960s.

Ralph Bunker, International Truck and Tractor dealer during the 1920s and 30s, was located at 67 Fifth Street. In the 1940s Von Cogswell (right) continued to operate at this location until his retirement in 1978.

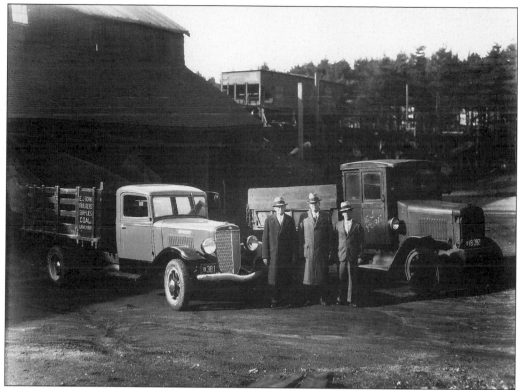

E.J. York established a coal business in 1893 with coal packets on Locust Street, having a capacity of five thousand tons on the B & M railroad spur. In 1897, a grain elevator was erected on Folsom Street. York also operated timber lots in New Hampshire and Maine. In 1915, his company cut five million feet of lumber.

During the early 1900s, James Parle established his ice business. John Grady later managed and then owned the Parle Ice business. As the demand for ice declined in the 1950s, the business began to deliver coal and oil.

Tuttle Square

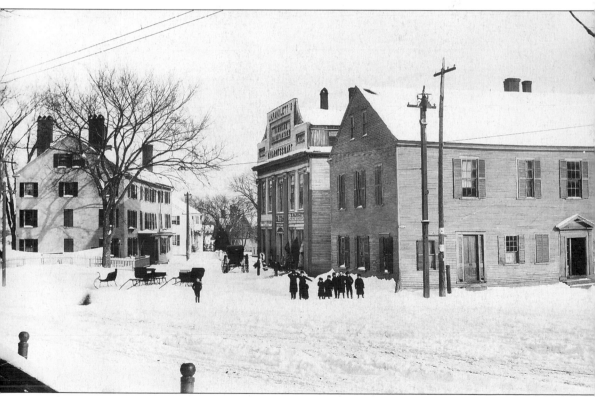

'The Corner' was the center of Dover's civic activities in the late 1700s and early 1800s. Wyatts Inn, also later called Dover Hotel, entertained President Monroe and General Lafayette. President John Quincy Adams also passed through here. In 1792, Dover was the state capital for one year and the old court house is where the legislature met. Built in 1789, the court house was also where the first Sunday school (Congregational) was held in 1818 and the first Catholic Mass in 1826.

Founded in 1864 on Locust Street, Randlett moved to the old Belleview Hall (built in 1834) to produce carriages of every description. Around 1905, the business became Dover Carriage Company.

Built in 1789 as the original court house, this building was turned into tenements in 1845 and later became Bradley Garage. It was torn down in 1924.

This photograph shows how building use changed with the times as the carriage shop became a garage for automobiles. Dover Garage (court house building) was torn down a year after this photograph was taken. A Mobil gas station now occupies the spot.

Frank's Jenny station was a popular service garage in Tuttle Square. The building is now home to Century 21 Real Estate.

Charles Newman started his apothecary business in the early 1900s. For many years, Newman's Pharmacy, located at 1 Silver Street, was one of the seven stores located in the square. The building was recently purchased by the First Parish Church.

This building was originally a single-bay Shell garage in the 1930s. It was known as Couture's Shell in this photograph during the 1950s. The garage still operates, now as Bob's Gulf.

56

Wentworth Garage. Governor Sherman Adams and family received a new car from Ray Wentworth at his 6 Milk Street garage in 1951. The Wentworth family also operated the Wentworth Bus Line. In March 1965 Kimball's Garage moved into the building.

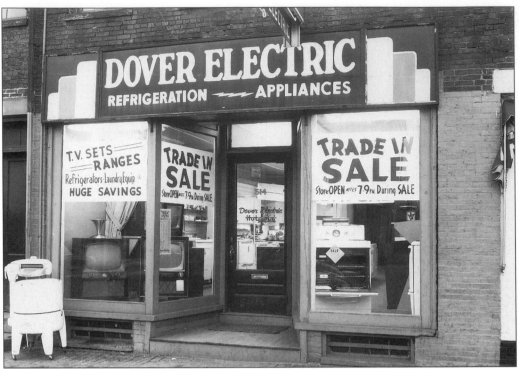

Dover Electric, at 514 Central Avenue, and S.D. Sundeen, located at 314 Central Avenue, were Dover's appliance centers during the 1950s. Sanfrid Sundeen opened in 1938 under the Belknap Church and later moved to a modern building next door where the family operated the business until 1984.

Coldbath Brothers. A turn-of-the-century meat provisions store was located at street level under the Belknap Church. S.D. Sundeen moved here in 1938.

Dover Grocery was located in Central Square on Washington Street. The building was replaced in 1895 by the Strafford Bank building.

Cartland's Grocery was located on Locust Street with a 40-foot frontage and 3,200 square feet of floor space, making it the largest grocery store in the city. Nine delivery wagons serviced customers. Mr. Cartland was considered one of Dover's most successful businessmen at the turn of the century.

Clark's Market was established in the late 1930s by John Clark on the corner of Mill Street and Central Avenue near Sawyer mills. These photographs were taken in 1951.

Joseph Newsky started his neighborhood market in the 1930s at 70 Waldron Street. In the 1950s Helen and Walter Newsky continued to operate the market serving the Washington Street area until urban renewal took over the neighborhood in the 1970s.

Raoul Roux moved his grocery business from lower Main Street to this location in the late 1930s and continued to operate The Corner Market into the 1960s.

P. Dillon Grocery was established in June 1905 at 270 Central Avenue. A leading dealer in grocery and kitchen supplies, Dillon had a reputation for first class goods, fair dealing and low prices.

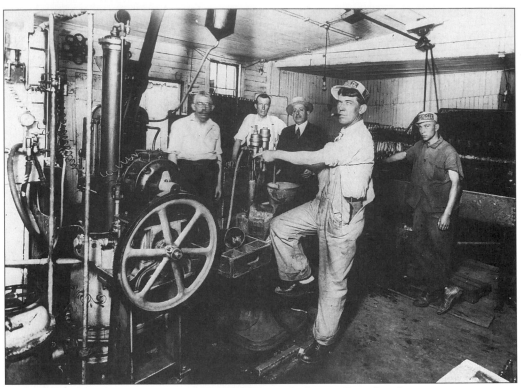

Robinson Bros. bottling company was established in May of 1898. Tom Robinson, Andrew Robinson, Tom O'Neil, William Robinson and Charles Mallen are seen here operating the bottling equipment.

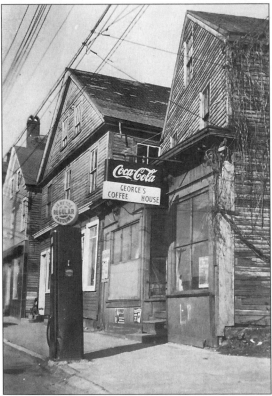

This photograph shows George's popular Greek Coffee House, Robinson Brothers and Janetos Market as they appeared on Main Street in the 1940s and '50s.

Two
Industry

"When you think of belts.
think of"
I.B.WILLIAMS & SONS
OAK TANNED LEATHER BELTING.

I.B. Williams was established in 1842 as part of the Cocheco Manufacturing Company and made belting for the mills. In 1871 Frank B. Williams was admitted into partnership with his father and the firm became I.B. Williams & Sons.

In 1874, property was acquired on Orchard Street and in 1878 George Williams was added to the firm and additional property was purchased. A substantial four-story brick building with a five-story tower was erected.

ESTABLISHED 1842
I.B. WILLIAMS & SONS
F.B.WILLIAMS, PROP.
TANNERS AND MANUFACTURERS OF

TEXTILE MILL BELTING.

E have made a special study of the belting needs of the textile manufacturer, aiming to produce special belting which shall give maximum service and results in this special work.

We furnish Cocheco Belting for the ordinary service and Shedite Waterproof Belting for the wet drives. Cocheco is an extra heavy belt of carefully selected oak-tanned, centre stock leather, put together with the utmost care and skill, and is guaranteed to transmit more power, with less loss from any cause, and do it longer than any other belt.

Shedite is exactly the same as Cocheco in quality, but is specially treated to make it waterproof and steamproof. Dampness, dripwater, steam-filled rooms, etc., have no effect on it unless to make it cling more closely to the pulley.

Write for catalog and full particulars.

FACTORY AT DOVER, N. H.
BRANCHES:
NEW YORK   CHICAGO   BOSTON
Agents in the larger cities in the United States and foreign countries.

In 1898 the Cocheco Manufacturing Company covered over 30 acres of floor space, operating 130,000 spindles in 2,800 looms. It required the labor of over 2,000 workers and the average wage was 53 cents per day. The bottom photograph was taken from the top of the old smokestack on Main Street.

Fifteen buildings were constructed between 1842 and 1844 on land that is now Henry Law Park. By the 1880s the Cocheco Print Works were renowned worldwide. Sixteen print machines as well as bleachery and finishing mills produced over 65,000 yards of cloth a year. In 1909, machinery was removed to Lawrence, Massachusetts, headquarters of the Pacific Mills (new owners) and the buildings were torn down in 1913.

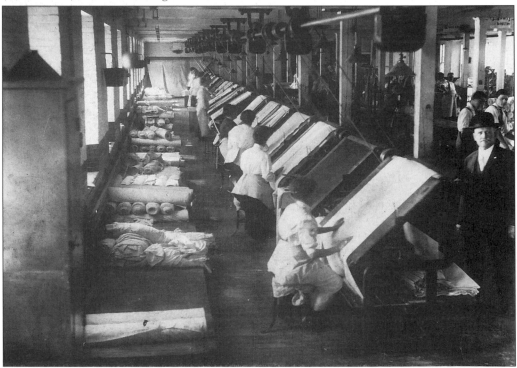

This view was taken from the roof of the granite Strafford Bank building and shows the area that is now Henry Law Park and Mill No. 1 in the left rear corner. In early years, some merchants occupied spaces in the foreground on Washington Street.

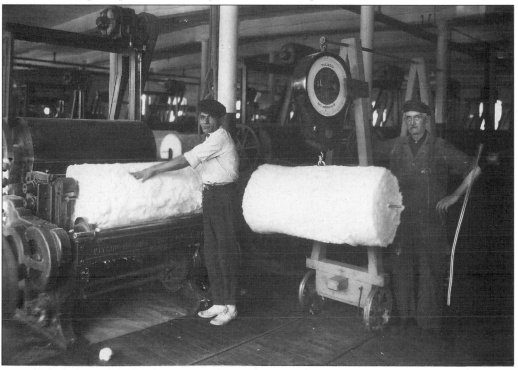

Pacific Mills took over in 1909 until a decline caused a shutdown in 1940. The mills were sold to the city by auction in 1941. A mill committee leased space to smaller industries such as Miller Shoe and Eastern Air Devices.

For many years during the city ownership of the mills, shoe manufacturing occupied much of the mill complex. After extensive renovations the old mills are now seeing activity again as offices for several businesses.

An early M & M Bakery truck with proprietor McManus standing with a loaf of his bread.

The Third Street factory was built in 1927 with a bread department, a cake department, and a dough room. Over one hundred trucks delivered to customers throughout New England.

Many local families had fresh 'Oven-Glo' bread on the table each day, until 1961 when the bakery finally closed.

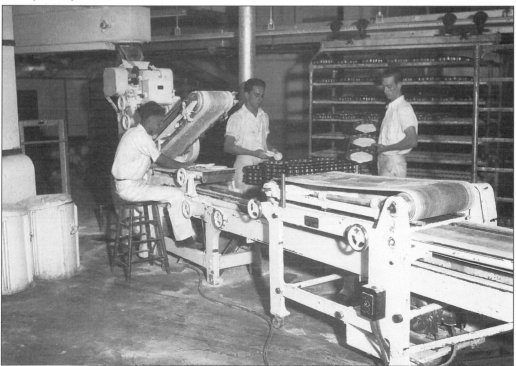

Mr. Dunaway founded Expello in 1928 at 15 Fourth Street. Around 1940, he moved to 6 Grove Street producing 'Expello,' a moth repellent, and 'Vanish' toilet bowl cleaner. In 1945, the business became Judson Dunaway Corporation, which continued until 1958. In 1965 the building became Northern Heel Co.

The Vulco unit box toe process patent was obtained on 13 August, 1913 by H.H. Beckwith. In 1916, Beckwith Manufacturing produced two hundred thousand pairs daily.

A photograph of Kidder Press Co. on Broadway taken in 1957 shows the large addition added to the older original buildings.

In 1899 Samuel Moore acquired Kidder Press, a printing process and business forms production equipment manufacturer. These photographs show workers in the 1930s.

Clarostat was a manufacturer of guaranteed performance potentiometers for industrial, military and service replacement applications from 1949 onwards. The factory recently closed (1993), when production was moved to Mexico. Old Mill No. 1 is currently undergoing extensive renovations for business and office use.

Sawyer's Lower Mill was home to the Dover Film Company in the late 1940s, producing roll film, motion picture film and a 'Dover Camera.' The factory has since been used for making shoes and currently houses Holmwood wood products.

As Dover continues to grow and attract business, the need for additional space gives birth to such initiatives as Enterprise Park.

Three
Municipal Services

Wentworth Hospital was founded in 1904 when Arioch Wentworth willed the city of Dover $100,000 to erect a forty-two bed cottage-type hospital. This photograph was taken in 1911.

This photograph was taken in 1944. Both this, and the previous photograph show the original buildings as they survived expansion and growth during this period of time.

In the 1960s, renovation to the hospital took place as seen in the above photograph.

Dr. O'Gara conducted classes in the old Rollins Building (built in 1922) which was used as a nursing school until 1952.

Dr. Edna Walck (center), Mayor Keefe (right) and Miss Hall, Hospital Director (left) pose with a group of Red Cross trainees/graduates on the steps of the Rollins Building.

In 1956, a fiftieth reunion of nurses at the hospital was held. This photograph was taken on the porch of the Rollins Building, the only structure of the early hospital to survive.

This photograph was taken in 1988 and shows an even greater expansion as the main entrance has been moved to the rear of the building.

The Wentworth Home was dedicated on 25 June, 1898, in honor of Arioch Wentworth who, in 1887, generously donated $10,000 towards construction and an additional $20,000 for a permanent fund. The home continues to operate with thirty-six ladies in residence.

Police Chief Murphy (center) poses with Gus Corn (left) and Paul Proux (right) in this 1950s photograph.

Police Chief Reynold (center) poses with Capt. Gary DeColfmacker (left) and Officer Charles 'Chuck' Maglaras (right) in this 1990s photograph.

Police cruisers and other city vehicles on the High School lawn for an annual report photograph.

Dare Officer Mark Leno stands with the Dare vehicle, refurbished from an old army ambulance.

A new Strafford County Court house was built in 1890 to replace space lost in the 1889 City Hall fire. It was constructed on the site of the old Waldron Garrison. Offices for all county officials and judges plus a three hundred-seat court room were used until 1974.

At the turn of the century, mail was delivered from this building (Union Block) on Washington Street. Littlefield, Frary and Co. hardware, E.J. York Coal and J.S. Abbott's office can be seen in this photograph.

Construction of the new Post Office building was completed in 1909. Many additions and changes have been made since, with a recent interior entrance renovation completed in August 1994.

The home of William Hale, Jr., a hardware merchant, was donated by the Trustees of the Franklin Academy when Andrew Carnegie gave $30,000 for the construction of a Public Library, which opened in July 1904.

Built in 1865, the Orchard Street Station (now the Firehouse Restaurant) was considered one of the neatest, coziest and best equipped engine houses in the state at the turn of the century.

This building was erected on land purchased in 1899 from the Broadway Baptist Church. A church building was moved across the street. By 1905 Broadway Station had one steam engine, one hook and ladder, and a hose wagon.

Fred Gilpatrick, Raymond Houde, Joe McCarthy, Fred Pinkham, Les Williams and Ray McKenney were familiar faces at the Dover Fire Department for many years.

Engine No. 4, now privately owned, can still be seen on occasion driving through town.

Dover Point Volunteer Fire Co. in January 1944. The driver in this photograph is Francis 'Bud' Stevens. In 1910, the building was erected to house a hand-drawn American La France chemical engine. In the 1940s, the station was part of the Civil Defense System with an air raid siren.

In 1939, the truck at Dover Point was made up from the body of an old Reo and a Dodge Bros. chassis and equipped with 600 feet of $2\frac{1}{2}$-inch canvas hose and a 400-gallon tank. In 1944, it was used to fill back pumps. The driver in this photograph is Captain Ernest Kluesener. The company was disbanded around 1956.

The original Cataract 4 (a hand tub) was established at Sawyer Mills in 1883 (Cataract Avenue was named after this unit.) Engine No. 3 was located at the corner of Central Avenue and Rutland Street.

Three Ahrens Fox trucks were purchased: a 1921 750 G.P.M. pumper, a 1924 hook and ladder, and a 1925 1,000 G.P.M. pumper.

On 26 January, 1907, Box 9 sounded at Mill No. 1. The fire resulted in a million dollar loss and four lives lost. Fireman battled the flames for thirty-six hours in –30 degree weather. The photograph below shows a front view.

Above, a hose crew streams water from the roof of the boiler house to cool the ruins. Below, ice covers the walls on the end of the ell of Mill No. 1, known today as the Clarostat Mill.

On the morning of 22 March, 1889, the City Hall was destroyed by fire, also causing damage to the spire of the adjoining Belknap Church.

On 29 March, 1906, the Masonic Temple in Central Square (at the same location as the above photograph) was destroyed by fire, destroying twenty-five businesses. The structure was rebuilt in 1907 at a cost of $75,000.

Early on the morning of 3 August, 1933, a fire was discovered at City Hall by a patrolman, and Box 31 sounded. Known as one of the finest municipal buildings in New England, it also had the largest stage in New Hampshire. By the end of the day only a shell was left standing. Many historic city records were lost.

Built in September 1914, St. Charles School experienced an explosion and fire during recess on 10 April, 1968. The building was demolished in December of the same year.

At 12:30 a.m. on 8 February, 1989, fire broke out in St. Mary's Hall on Chestnut Street. This photograph was taken at 7:30 a.m. showing the total loss by that hour.

On 3 January, 1932, at 11:40 p.m. Box 13 was rung. Thirty-seven men with equipment arrived in 55 minutes from Haverhill, Massachusetts as the call for assistance was sent. Twenty-six firms and one hundred people were left jobless as the morning light shone on the ashes of what was the Morrill Block. The only business that survived was the Tasker and Chesley Funeral Home.

Founded in 1933 by Sidney Robbins, the Washington Street automobile parts business was destroyed by fire in April 1950. Rebuilt from ashes, the Robbins family now operates eleven stores around the state.

Four
Schools

The original High School was built in 1851 for students living on the north side of the river. In 1869, consolidation of the school system allowed all Dover students to attend classes, with eighty in attendance. Railroad expansion made the location at the end of First Street a poor one and the school was torn down to make room for the Eastern States Warehouse.

GRADUATING EXERCISES

❧ OF THE ❧

❧ HIGH SCHOOL, ❧

DOVER, N. H.,

AT CITY OPERA HOUSE,

AT TWO AND ONE-HALF O'CLOCK,

THURSDAY AFTERNOON, JUNE 21, 1900.

A new High School was built in 1902 to accommodate the growing school population. A faculty group poses on the lawn as the camera captures many familiar faces in 1946.

The Dover High Orchestra (*c.* 1927) and the 1948 Dover High Band pose for yearbook photographs on the steps of City Hall.

The Dover High senior play group (*c.* 1928) and the 1957 queen's court are also captured by the yearbook photographer.

Dover has always had active sports programs through the years. These photographs show the 1936 girls' basketball and football teams. Coach Adams (top photograph) was a familiar face on the Dover sports scene for many years.

The Sawyer School was built in
1870 at a cost of $30,000 with eight
classrooms for 192 pupils. It was
named for the Hon. Thomas E.
Sawyer, who was intimately
connected with Dover schools for
half a century. On 30 June, 1979,
irreparable damage to the school was
caused when overheated wiring
resulted in a major fire.

The Sawyer class of 1896 (above) and 1946 (below) pose for their graduation portraits on the front steps of the school.

Pine Hill School, built in 1824, was half primary and half secondary. By 1904, only the fifth and sixth grades were taught to forty students. The school was abandoned in 1905 and torn down in 1913. The site is at the entrance to Pine Hill cemetery.

The Sherman School was built in 1828 and named in honor of its first headmaster, Enoch Sherman. The upper floor was reserved for advanced classes. The school was damaged during the hurricanes of 1938.

Mary Elizabeth Peirce, D.H.S. class of
1893, taught at the Varney School,
designated in 1890 as a training school
for high school graduates wishing to
become teachers. Miss Peirce is shown
below with her third grade class.

This school was built in 1861 as the Washington Street Primary School. In 1882, the school was renamed the Varney School, in honor of Judge John Varney, a school board member killed in the Baptist Church fire in 1882. The school closed in 1953 and became a law office in 1958.

Known as the Locust Street Primary School and later the Hale School, this building had four levels of primary education. Classes moved to Woodman Park School in 1953. The building is presently being used as a law office.

Belknap School was built in 1855 on the site of Jeremy Belknap's house (where the famous *History of New Hampshire* was written.) It was used as a grade school until 1953 when its students also moved to Woodman Park School.

116

Woodman Park School was the largest elementary school in the state when it was opened in 1953. Seated for this photograph are members of the original faculty.

After a fire destroyed the Dover Industrial School, located in the basement of the Opera House, vocational education was moved to an old mill building on Main Street and was known as Davis Vocational.

Sheet metal, electronics, machine shop and auto repair were popular trades taught at the school for many years.

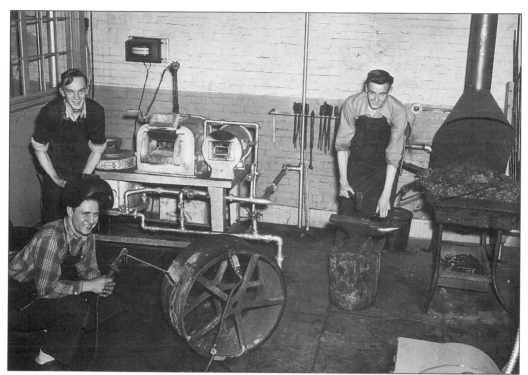

Welding and cosmetology courses were also offered at Davis Vocational. The school is currently a private office building.

Dover Industrial School was located in the basement of the old City Hall. Classes were offered for both girls and boys, teaching skills such as drafting, woodworking, cooking and ironing.

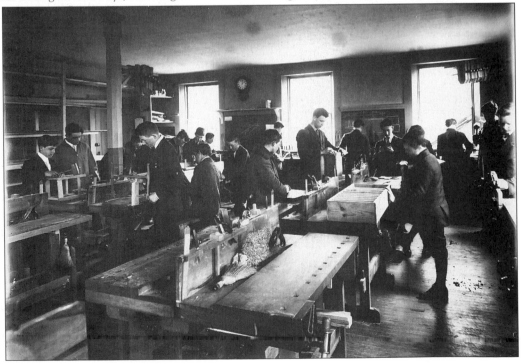

Saint Mary High School girls present 'Hayride' at the Dover City Hall Auditorium.

Saint Charles School was built in 1914 at a cost of $20,000 for forty students who were taught by the Sisters of Presentation.

Built in 1888, Saint Joseph's Boys School had 230 boys enrolled by 1898. It became an apartment house and was eventually removed for parking space at the present Saint Charles Church.

Dover Business College was founded in 1896 and run by the McIntosh brothers at 99 Washington Street. In 1936, McIntosh College was located at Orchard Street offering day and evening business courses. In 1970, the school was moved to a new facility at 23 Cataract Avenue.

Formerly an armory building, the Ida B. Hanson Elementary School was named after a Belknap School teacher-principal. The school was located at St. Thomas Street behind the High School. Below, Myrtle Allen's 1937 class poses on the steps.

Lothrop Memorial Hall was built in 1916 as a memorial to Dr. James Lothrop, to be used as a recreational hall. Many of Dover's youth played basketball in this hall until 1938 when the Lebanese community purchased the building, which is now called St. George's Church.

National Guard Armory Battery B Basketball Team in 1936.

Battery B Basketball Team in 1949.

State Champions, Barrington Orioles Baseball Team leave for Kansas on 11 August, 1938. The team placed fifth in the country. Star athlete, coach and former superintendent of Dover schools Fred Walker stands in the center of the photograph.

Five

Homes

'My Friends: This old garrison which you see so well cared for, both for the present and future, I have worked for and studied the needs of, for more than thirty years. It has become very dear to me.

It now gives me pleasure to place it in the care of the trustees of the Woodman Institute. I do this, not for the honor of giving, but for the benefit of the public in my day and after I am gone, and I hope it may be received by the public in as kindly a spirit as it is given.'

Mrs. Ellen S. Rounds,
Donor of the Garrison House, July 1916.

As many as eighteen garrisons were believed to exist in the Dover area, 'The Garrison City.' Preserved at the Woodman Institute Museum is the only surviving garrison, once located at Back River and known as the Damm Garrison. Annie Woodman bequeathed $100,000 in 1915 for the establishment of a natural science and history museum which operates to this day and is free to the public.

Built in 1690 and known as Captain Heard Farm, this property was purchased by sea captain James Guppy in 1767 and remained in the Guppy family for 150 years. The Guppy House was left to the city of Dover by Jeremy Belknap Guppy but was destroyed by fire in 1952.

Built in 1695 by Ebenezer Varney and purchased by John Ham in 1846, the Ham-Varney Home was located at the base of Garrison Hill near Varney Street.

The Cressey-Hale Home was built by Stephen Hanson in 1807 and purchased by George Folsom (oil-paint dealer) in 1851. Later it went to J.B. Folsom (oil-cloth factory owner) until 1876 when Thaddeus Cressey (millinery shop owner) lived here. Eva Cressey Hale occupied the residence in the early 1900s. The land was eventually donated by the Carberry family for the construction of a new Catholic Church in 1946.

This home was built by attorney Henry Mellen in the 1790s. In 1822, Andrew Pierce purchased the home for $1,835. Pierce became Dover's first mayor in 1855 at the age of seventy. In 1880 G. Fisher Piper owned the house and divided it in half: one side for he and his wife, and the other for his two schoolteacher sisters Mary and Sarah. The Piper House still stands on Silver Street.

Sawyer's Mansion was a twenty-six room home built during the Civil War at a cost of $250,000. A five-story front tower was added in 1885. It was situated on 17 acres with stables, a carriage house, a fruit orchard and a greenhouse all built for Jonathan Sawyer of the Sawyer Mills. Hollywood producer Busby Berkley lost ownership when the city acquired the property for back taxes and sold it at auction in 1943. Unfortunately the mansion was torn down during the construction of the Spaulding Turnpike and a Howard Johnsons was erected. A Burger King restaurant now occupies the site.

Once a model dairy farm and home to Governor Charles Sawyer, Green Pastures was a nursing home during the 1950s and '60s. Now the house is a private residence located on Dover Point Road.

Built in 1827, the Governor Noah Martin Home on Nelson Street was purchased by the Martin family in 1835. Dr. Martin was elected Governor in 1852 on the Democratic ticket. He was the founder of the Dover Medical Society.

Dr. Levi Hill moved to Dover in 1848. He served as President of the Dover Medical Society in 1854 and President of the New Hampshire Medical Society in 1869. The house was removed to build the post office.

Six
Churches

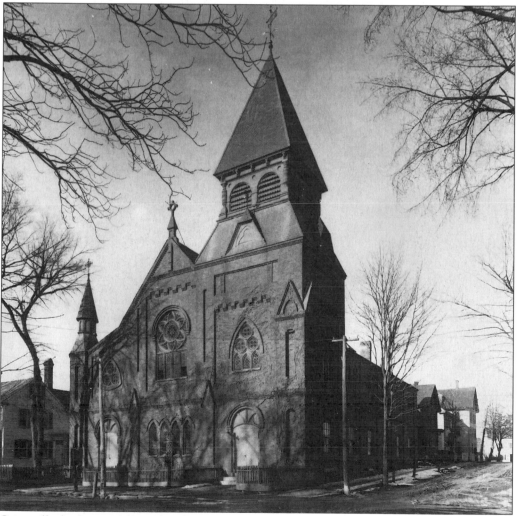

Originally built in 1869, a fire destroyed this structure in 1882. The present building was dedicated on 22 March, 1883. Additions have been made in recent years.

Built in 1768, the Friends Meeting House is the oldest church building in Dover. The first meeting of the Society of Friends was at Dover Neck around 1680. This meeting house was used as a receiving station in the underground railroad during the Civil War and in 1804 the parents of John Greenleaf Whittier were married here.

A solemn opening at Temple Israel was held on 14 November, 1938. Members of the community marched from their rented rooms next to Fosters, carrying the Torahs and flags to their new house of worship. Renovations were dedicated on 20 September, 1970.

134

The Central Avenue Freewill Baptist Church was built in 1828 on land given by the Cocheco Manufacturing Company. Later it became Flowers Furniture, then Monarch Diner, and finally Dunkin' Donuts.

This interior view of the First Parish Congregational Church (built in 1829) shows the balcony seating on side walls which were removed in the 1940s.

The Advent Christian Church was dedicated on 16 April, 1832 on the corner of Atkinson and St. Thomas Streets. This photograph was taken c. 1906. In 1978, a new church was erected on Sixth Street. The old building is now home to the Dover Adult Learning Center.

The Adventists were believers in the second coming of Christ and the doctrine of Millerism founded by preacher William Miller in 1842.

Pictured here are Rev. Dunstan's choir (*c.* 1930s) and, below, Rev. Blankenship's (*c.* 1960s) at St. Thomas Church. The stone church opened on the first Sunday in September 1892. The church was designed by Boston architect Henry Vaughn.

St. Mary's is the oldest active Catholic parish in New Hampshire. This second building was dedicated in 1872 after the first structure, built in 1828, was destroyed by fire.

In 1947 the heavy cornice and crosses on the tower were removed and replaced with a new roof and a single cross.

The original St. Thomas Church was built in 1840 next to the Hale House on Central Avenue. The church was torn down and the house moved across the street to its present location in 1891, to make room for a new City Hall.

St. Charles Church was completed 8 November, 1896, and destroyed by fire in 1932. Replaced in 1933 with a new church located on Central Avenue, the Convent (foreground) is now the Dover Senior Center.

The First Unitarian Church was built in 1828 on Locust Street after a doctrinal split from the First Parish Church developed. In 1865, Hon. John P. Hale delivered his last address in Dover prior to his departure to Spain. In 1939, the Greek Community purchased the property. The building was destroyed by fire in December 1956.

St. Joseph's Church held the first Mass celebration at Christmas in 1946. Monsignor Charles J. Leddy was the first pastor.

Bishop Matthew F. Brady, D.D., officiated at the dedication on 12 October, 1948.

The Universalist Church, known as the Peirce Memorial (organized 1837), was built on land donated by Thomas W. Peirce and named in 1880 in memory of his parents. When the Locust Street Church closed many parishioners joined the Peirce Church, located at the corner of Peirce Street and Central Avenue. The building was torn down in 1976.

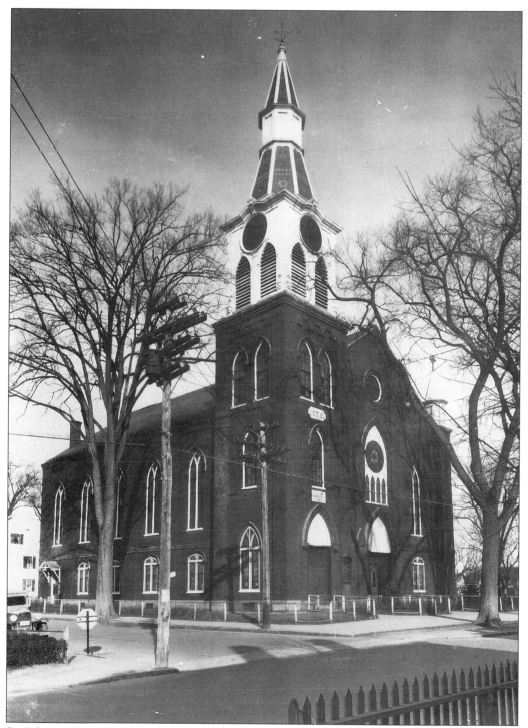

St. John's Methodist Church was built in 1875 and became the second church in America to have chimes. Faced with a need for extensive renovations and a lack of parking in the 1960s, a new church was erected on Cataract Avenue in 1970. The old church building is now senior citizen housing.

In 1856, some conservative members of First Parish formed a second congregational church. On 4 July, 1859, the cornerstone of the Belknap Church (named after Rev. Jeremey Belknap) was laid. Damaged by the City Hall fire in 1889, then again during the Masonic Temple fire in 1906, it finally closed in 1911. However, the Belknap Society continued until November 1963 when the remaining members voted to disband. The church was razed in 1965 to make way for parking.

Seven
Moving Pictures

The Clement Theatre was one of Dover's early moving picture theatres. Located on the second floor of the Old Broadway Baptist Church building, it had been moved across the street to make room for the Broadway Fire Station.

JUST THIS ONCE

—GO TO THE—

OPERA HOUSE

And see a programme of

MOVING PICTURES

AND ILLUSTRATED SONGS

That is the best in New England.   All Feature Pictures.

FRIDAY AND SATURDAY ONLY

A Heart Touching Drama,

A Pair of White Gloves. 1062 Ft. Long

Edison's Latest Features,

THE ROAD TO LOVE
AND LUNATICS IN POWER

NEW SONGS BY MISS MILDRED PRESCOTT

The Broadway Theatre was operated by Jesse Bridgham from the late 1930s until a fire in 1945 destroyed the building. It was reopened as the Uptown.

The Orpheum Theatre opened in 1912 on Washington Street. It was known as the Orpheum Hotel for many years.

The Orpheum became the State in 1936 and closed around 1955.

In this photograph a crowd gathers for a showing of an early sex education film.

The Strand was built in 1919 in the style of the Strand theatre in London. Opening night was 22 September, 1919 and featured 'Daddy Long Legs,' starring Mary Pickford with full orchestra accompaniment. In 1929 the first of the 'talkies' shown in the state was here on modern sound equipment. After many exterior changes, Michael Spinelli completely renovated and restored the Strand with a gala grand re-opening on 22 September, 1987.

A standard monkey business film with good special effects (it won an Academy Award) got top billing in 1949 when Joe came to Dover.

'Like Popeye eats his spinach, I eat my Quaker Oats to give pepum for laffen in my latest feature picture 'Six Day Bike Ride'-Joe E. Brown.

The Soap Box Derby was once an annual event in Dover. Bruce Dearborn, the local winner in 1949, was off to the National in Akron, Ohio.

The original Children's Home (10 May, 1893) was located in a tenement at 8 Atkinson Street and later on 11 Spring Street. Designed by A.T. Ramsdell of Dover, the cornerstone on the Locust street home was laid on Saturday 9 October, 1897. In the late '20s, as many as sixty children lived at the home.

Mr. Henry Law was present in August 1937 to dedicate the gift of a new outdoor pool to the city.

Many Dover children learned to swim and enjoyed Bellamy Park during the summer of 1949.

Charles Howe came to Dover in 1891. Between 1893 and 1901, he erected fourteen glass greenhouses, covering 5 acres of land at the base of Garrison Hill. This became the largest greenhouse complex in the state. A hurricane in November 1950 destroyed most of the complex.

In 1880, a 65-foot wooden observatory was built by Harrison Haley, modeled on a similar structure at Coney Island. The tower was five stories high with a mansard roof and open balconies on every floor. A 10 cent admission was charged to climb to the top. Over 6,000 tickets were sold the first year. A restaurant at the base offered light lunches and cold drinks. On 27 June, 1897, a careless smoker's match destroyed the tower.

GARRISON HILL AND THE OBSERVATORY.

DOVER, N. H.

The hill rises above the City nearly 300 feet, and is one mile from the City Hall. Garrison is the name given to the hill from the garrisons built there during the old French and Indian wars, by which Dover as a frontier town suffered severely.

The Old House at the foot of the hill was built in 1680, which was spared distruction by the savages that befell other houses of its time.

This hill has been for many years past a favorite resort with tourists.

The late Hon. John P. Hale on his return from Europe, said in a public address, " That of the hills he had visited in any country, none for beauty and variety of scenery surpasses Garrison Hill." About six acres of this hill are covered with a fine grove, with walks, seats, swings, &c. A most desirable place for Picnics.

THE OBSERVATORY.

Was built in the autumn of 1880. Its construction is similar to the one at Coney Island, N. Y., and that on Davis' Hill, Philadelphia, with open balconies, so as to afford unobstructed views. The highest balcony affords a view of rare beauty, characteristic of New Hampshire; the great distant ring of the horizon is rugged and broken with a continuous chain of hills, save when, in the south, the distant ocean shows his line of blue.

In the east is the ever beautiful Agamenticus, the Sentinel of the Sea; northeast is " Boneg Beag" in North Berwick; a little more to the north are the mountains of western Maine in and near Farmington; then the eye rests upon the stately peaks of the White Mountain range, clear and blue, in the far north. The Summit House on Mount Washington, a distance of 90 miles, is distinctly seen with the aid of a glass on a clear day. Turning westward the eye meets some lofty faint peaks of the Franconia Range, probably " Lafayette" and the " Haystacks," bearing a little west of north.— Below these and nearer, the graceful pyramid of the North Conway " Kearsarge" is seen in relief. The Chocorua's lofty peak is also conspicuous.— Northwest are the heights of the Sandwich Dome and the Ossipee range; westward are seen the neighbors' Blue Job and Strafford Ridge; while the Saddle Back and Nottingham Hills in the southwest complete the mountain circle. Due south is old ocean, sleeping in a line of sunny haze and flecked with snowy sails. Conspicuous above the southern sky-line is the palatial " Wentworth" at Newcastle; beyond, the Isles of Shoals, even the dashing waves against its rocky shores are visible at times.

The spires of the City of Portsmouth, the light-houses on the coast and the Navy Yard are within view. Occasional water views purify the beauty of the nearer landscape, afforded by the Piscataqua, Exeter and Cocheco rivers; the Great Bay at Greenland, while the view of the western meadows and woodland, clad in Nature's eternal robes of peace and harmonious beauty, is unsurpassed. Gazing upon scenery thus charming, one is reminded of Whittier's beautiful lines:

" Touched by a light that never dies.
A glory never sung,
Aloft on sky and mountain wall
Are God's great pictures hung."

In the Tower is a POWERFUL TELESCOPE, Free to the use of all Visitors.

☞ The first story of the Tower is fitted up for a Restaurant.

☞ An Omnibus runs regularly to the Hill.

M. J. SMITH,

Bracewell Building,

Photographic Work of Every Description.

Water Colors and Crayons.

PICTURE FRAMING TO ORDER.

July and August

excursion and vacation months for most people, are of all the year, the months when the most outside photographic work is done.

But the photographer who depends upon straight portrait work for his business, finds these two months the dullest of the year. To stimulate business at this time, we have in the past tried various ideas with more or less success.

This year we propose to **Advertise** by placing a limited amount of new work directly in the hands of customers, at what might be called a "Bargain Counter Price."

Since the actual average cost of making the **first** cabinet photograph (not counting time or labor), is considerably more than the 50 cents asked, it is plain that this scheme without re-orders will be a losing venture. While we shall consider no one under the slightest obligation to take more than the one photo, still we shall make every endeavor to make that one **so pleasing,** that sooner or later you cannot resist the temptation to place a re-order.

If your last Portraits, wherever made, were not entirely satisfactory, we should be pleased to try you on these terms.

A new costume, a becoming hat, a growing child, a gift to a friend, a graduation dress (with or without diploma), are among the many reasons why you should take advantage of this offer.

If this scheme does not interest you at present, will you kindly hand this letter and coupon to some one who may wish to use it now? Only a few of these will be issued, good not later than July 31st, and an equal number for August.

Yours respectfully,

Smith, the Photographer,

Suite 12, Bracewell Building,   *DOVER, N. H.*

Acknowledgements

Credits for making this book possible would first and foremost have to go to the photographers whose negatives were used to reproduce these historical images. They did not realize at the time what a valuable resource their photographs would become:

M.J. Smith; Norman Seavey; A. Thornton Gray; J. Edward Rivers; Andrew 'Andy' Rivers; and George Wentworth.

Reference Material:

Dover Public Library, Woodman Institute, Dover Heritage Group

Special Thanks:

Robert Whitehouse (author) *Port of Dover*
Lynne Wissink (author) *The Marlinspike*

A very special thanks to my son Jason for his research and computer assistance in making this book a reality.